DOCUMENTING U.S. HISTORY

THE JOURNALS OF LEWIS AND CLARK

Darlene R. Stille

Chicago, Illinois

www.capstonepub.com
Visit our website to find out more information about Heinemann-Raintree books.

To order:
☎ Phone 800-747-4992
💻 Visit www.capstonepub.com to browse our catalog and order online.

Edited by Abby Colich, Megan Cotugno, and Laura Hensley
Designed by Cynthia Della-Rovere
Original illustrations © Capstone Global Library Limited 2011
Illustrated by Oxford Designers & Illustrators
Picture research by Tracy Cummins
Originated by Capstone Global Library Limited
Printed and bound in China by CTPS

16 15 14 13 12
10 9 8 7 6 5 4 3 2 1

Library of Congress Cataloging-in-Publication Data
Stille, Darlene R.
  The journals of Lewis and Clark / Darlene R. Stille.
    p. cm.—(Documenting U.S. history)
  Includes bibliographical references and index.
  ISBN 978-1-4329-6754-3 (hb)—ISBN 978-1-4329-6763-5 (pb) 1. Journals of the Lewis and Clark Expedition—Juvenile literature. 2. Lewis and Clark Expedition (1804-1806)—Juvenile literature. 3. West (U.S.)—Description and travel—Juvenile literature. 4. Lewis, Meriwether, 1774-1809—Diaries—Juvenile literature. 5. Clark, William, 1770-1838—Diaries—Juvenile literature. 6. Explorers—West (U.S.)—Diaries—Juvenile literature. I. Title.
  F592.7.S733 2012
  917.804'2—dc23   2011037783

Acknowledgments
The author and publishers are grateful to the following for permission to reproduce copyright material: to come

Alamy: pp. 21 (© North Wind Picture Archives), 35 (© North Wind Picture Archives); AP Photo: pp. 5 (Charles Rex Arbogast), 41 (Jacqueline Larma); Corbis: pp. 19 (© Blue Lantern Studio), 25 (© Blue Lantern Studio), 36 (© Lee Snider/Photo Images); Getty Images: pp. 4 (David David Gallery), 13 (Jean-Erick PASQUIER/Gamma-Rapho), 14 (Jean-Erick PASQUIER/Gamma-Rapho), 17 (Danita Delimont), 30 (Superstock), 43 (Mike Theiss); Library of Congress Prints and Photographs Division: pp. 9, 11; newscom: p. 26 (© Bill Greenblatt); Shutterstock: pp. 7 (© Neale Cousland), 15 (© Nelson Sirlin), 29 (© akva), 33 (© Scott E Read); The Granger Collection: pp. 10, 22, 23, 27, 28, 38.

Cover image of William Clark sketch of a trout in the Lewis and Clark expedition diary reproduced with permission from Alamy (© North Wind Picture Archives). Cover image of American explorers Meriwether Lewis (1774 - 1809) and William Clark (1770 - 1838) at the mouth of the Columbia River during their exploration of the Louisiana Territory painting by Frederic Remington reproduced with permission from Getty Images.

Every effort has been made to contact copyright holders of material reproduced in this book. Any omissions will be rectified in subsequent printings if notice is given to the publisher.

Disclaimer
All the Internet addresses (URLs) given in this book were valid at the time of going to press. However, due to the dynamic nature of the Internet, some addresses may have changed, or sites may have changed or ceased to exist since publication. While the author and publisher regret any inconvenience this may cause readers, no responsibility for any such changes can be accepted by either the author or the publisher.

Contents

Some words are printed in **bold**, like this. You can find out what they mean by looking in the glossary.

Recording Important Events

People make documents to record important events. These documents might tell about a war or how people lived. They might tell how a nation started. There are two kinds of historical documents. They are called **primary sources** and **secondary sources**.

Primary sources

A primary source could be made by someone who saw a historical event. It could also be made by someone who was actually involved in a historical event.

Primary sources could be letters or newspaper articles by reporters at the scene. They could be maps, drawings, photographs, or official documents, such as a constitution. Primary sources could also be diaries or **journals**.

The journals of Lewis and Clark are a primary source used by many to learn about their journey through the western United States.

This is a photo of inside pages of one of the journals written by U.S. explorers Meriwether Lewis and William Clark.

Two U.S. explorers, Meriwether Lewis and William Clark, wrote important journals. They tell about their journey northwest to explore **territory** bought by the United States in 1803.

Secondary sources

Secondary sources are made by people who did not see an event happen and did not take part in the event. Rather, these authors study history and primary sources and write about them. History books and encyclopedia articles are secondary sources. A book about a scientific discovery is a secondary source. Some websites can also be secondary sources. This book is a secondary source.

Using primary and secondary sources

Primary sources are an incredibly important tool for people who study history. They show how people lived and what they experienced in early historical periods. In particular, journals, such as those of Lewis and Clark, provide an insight into what people were thinking and feeling at a certain moment in history.

Secondary sources are also useful. They help people to better understand primary sources. Secondary sources may explain what a primary source means. Sometimes the writing in a primary source is hard to understand. If it was written long ago, it may contain words and expressions that people no longer use. This is often the case with the journals of Lewis and Clark. Secondary sources help explain why an event or document is important.

Know It!

Benjamin Franklin helped found the American Philosophical Society in 1743. Its members met to talk about medicine, science, and other topics. The society's members still meet twice a year. The original Lewis and Clark journals are housed in its building today.

Keeping primary sources safe

Librarians usually make sure that primary sources are safe. The documents must not get wet or torn. They must not be handled very much. They must be safe from fires and other disasters.

Library **vaults** are safe rooms that hold the most important primary sources. Vaults that store some of the most important documents in U.S. history are in the National **Archives** and the Library of Congress, both in Washington, D.C. The American Philosophical Society (APS), in Philadelphia, Pennsylvania, stores the Lewis and Clark journals. These places ensure that important pieces of history are preserved for future generations.

Important primary sources are kept in reading rooms, where people come to see them.

A Time of Expansion

In 1803 the United States was a new nation. Americans had declared independence from Great Britain only 27 years before. By 1803 Americans had elected three presidents. The current president was Thomas Jefferson (see the box).

A new nation

The new nation stretched westward from the Atlantic Ocean to the Mississippi River. North to south, it stretched from Canada to Florida (see the map).

Americans who lived west of the Appalachian Mountains grew more **produce** than they could use. Farmers sent produce, and traders sent furs, by boat down the Mississippi River to New Orleans, in present-day Louisiana. From there, the goods were shipped to Europe.

This map shows the United States in 1803, after the Louisiana Purchase (see page 10).

(see page 10)

1800
Spain promises the Louisiana Territory to France in a secret treaty.

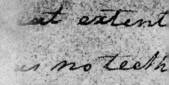

Know It!

The fur trade was big business in early North America. The Americans, British, and French competed to trap beaver furs. They also traded with American Indians for furs. In Europe beaver furs were made into hats.

Worried about foreign nations

President Jefferson had been interested in a huge area called the Louisiana **Territory** for a long time. Louisiana covered land from the Mississippi River northwest to the Rocky Mountains (see the map).

Spain owned Louisiana, but it had promised it to France in a secret **treaty** in 1800. Jefferson feared that France might try to block U.S. produce and furs from traveling freely through New Orleans.

Thomas Jefferson
(1743–1826)

Thomas Jefferson became the third U.S. president in 1801. A lawyer and **plantation** owner, Jefferson also loved science and nature. He wanted to learn about plants and animals in the Louisiana Territory. He wanted to learn about the American Indians who lived there.

1801
Thomas Jefferson becomes the third president of the United States.

France makes a deal

Emperor Napoleon I (see the box) was ruler of France in 1803. He planned to set up French **colonies** along the Mississippi River. He ordered an army to go to Louisiana. But the army never made it. Instead, the army was sent to the French colony of Haiti, in the Caribbean. Rebelling **slaves** there defeated the French Army.

Meanwhile, President Jefferson warned France not to take over Louisiana. Napoleon knew that France and Great Britain would soon be at war in Europe. He feared that the United States would join forces with Great Britain if he angered its leaders.

This painting shows the signing of the Louisiana Purchase by Marquis Francois de Barbe-Marbois, Robert Livingston, and James Monroe in Paris on April 30, 1803.

April 30, 1803
France sells the Louisiana Territory to the United States for $15 million.

The Louisiana Purchase

Napoleon decided it was best to sell Louisiana to the United States to keep peace with the young nation. So, in 1803, France sold the Louisiana Territory to the U.S. government. The price was $15 million. Overnight, the size of the United States had doubled (see the map on page 8).

Napoleon Bonaparte
(1769–1821)

Napoleon Bonaparte was a great military leader. He became a general in the French Army. During the 1790s, France was at war with most countries in Europe. Napoleon won victories in Europe and in the Middle East. He then seized control of the French government.

Napoleon dreamed of conquering Europe. In 1804 he crowned himself emperor of France. He used the money from selling the Louisiana Territory to help pay for his wars. At first Napoleon's army won great victories. But twice he suffered terrible defeats. British soldiers finally defeated Napoleon in the Battle of Waterloo in 1815, in present-day Belgium.

The Need to Explore the West

Now that the United States owned the Louisiana **Territory**, President Jefferson ordered an **expedition** to explore this vast new area of land.

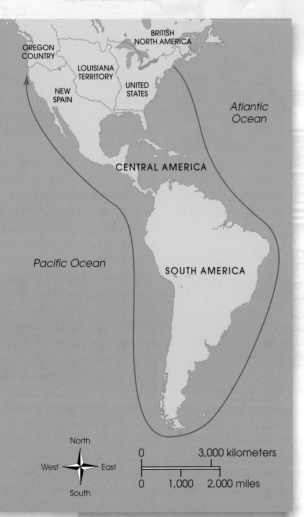

OREGON COUNTRY

BRITISH NORTH AMERICA

LOUISIANA TERRITORY

NEW SPAIN

UNITED STATES

Atlantic Ocean

CENTRAL AMERICA

Pacific Ocean

SOUTH AMERICA

North
West — East
South

0   3,000 kilometers

0   1,000   2,000 miles

Goals for the expedition

Jefferson had several goals for the expedition:

- He wanted scientific information about the plants and animals in the new territory.

- He wanted to find a river that ships could sail to get to the Pacific Ocean. At that time, ships had to sail around the tip of South America to reach the Pacific coast (see the map). Jefferson wanted to find the boundaries of the Louisiana Territory and see if there was a new, better route.

Early Americans took a very long route to the Pacific Ocean.

1803
Jefferson orders an expedition to explore the Louisiana Territory.

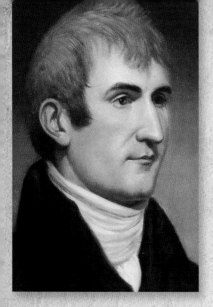

Meriwether Lewis (1774–1809)

When Jefferson began looking for volunteers to explore the West in 1792, Meriwether Lewis was one of the first to apply. But at age 18, Lewis was too young. So he joined the U.S. Army and learned to live in the wilderness of Ohio and Tennessee. He became a captain. By 1801, Lewis had the experience that Jefferson was looking for. Lewis then studied how to classify plants and animals. One of his jobs would be to collect **specimens** of plants, animals, and rocks.

- He wanted to expand the U.S. fur trade. Jefferson wanted to know which American Indians might be willing to trade furs for other goods.

- Finally, Jefferson wanted to claim Oregon Country (see the map on page 8) for the United States.

Choosing leaders

Jefferson chose Meriwether Lewis (see the box) as one of the expedition leaders. Lewis was Jefferson's private secretary. Lewis then chose William Clark (see page 14) to be another leader. Both men had served in the U.S. Army.

1803
Jefferson offers Meriwether Lewis the opportunity to lead the expedition.

1803
Lewis asks William Clark to join him on the expedition.

The little-known West

Lewis and Clark were very brave. They knew little about where they were heading. Much of what they knew came from fur trappers and traders. Traders traveled west along the Missouri River and other rivers. They brought back stories of a wild and beautiful land.

Lewis and Clark knew that winters would be cold, and that food would be hard to find in the winter. They knew they faced rugged mountains, but did not know how big they were. They knew American Indians lived on the land, but they did not know if they would be helpful or angry about their presence. They also did not know whether the land was filled with dangerous animals or poisonous plants.

William Clark
(1770–1838)

William Clark served in the U.S. Army. At one time, he was the commanding officer of Lewis. In 1796 Clark went home to Kentucky to regain his health. Lewis invited Clark to be coleader of the expedition to explore the Northwest. Lewis did not only value Clark as a leader. He also valued Clark as a skilled mapmaker. Clark would make the first detailed maps of the American West.

"The Sergt…will command the guard, manage the sails, see that the men at the oars do their duty…and that the boat gets under way in due time; he will keep a good lookout for the mouths of rivers, creeks, Islands, and other remarkable places and shall immediately report the same to the commanding officers."

—*Meriwether Lewis, May 26, 1804*

Lewis and Clark encountered a lot of rugged terrain on their expedition.

Setting off

The expedition needed careful planning. The explorers needed boats to travel rivers. They needed special supplies for surviving in the wilderness. They also needed people with outdoor skills.

Getting ready

Lewis went to Pennsylvania in 1803. He studied science with members of the American Philosophical Society (see page 7).

Lewis also bought supplies. He bought mosquito netting and beads for trading with American Indians. He also bought rifles and gunpowder so the explorers could hunt for food. Lewis had a 55-foot- (17-meter-) long **keelboat** made for the expedition. Sails or people rowing with oars can power a keelboat.

Clark was busy recruiting men for the expedition. He needed strong men who had lived in the wilderness. Most of the men he chose were soldiers, who would be used to working hard. They would also be used to obeying orders. He selected about 40 men for what became known as the Corps of Discovery.

1803
Lewis travels to Philadelphia to study science and other subjects and gather supplies in preparation for the expedition.

1803
Clark begins recruiting men for the expedition.

Training for the trip

Lewis sailed along the Ohio River toward the Mississippi River. Along the way, he picked up Clark and the recruits. They spent the winter of 1803–1804 at Camp Dubois, across from St. Louis. Lewis and Clark trained the men and learned all they could about the Missouri River. They were ready for their journey to begin.

Keelboats were large boats with flat bottoms used for traveling on shallow rivers.

winter 1803–1804
Lewis, Clark, and their crew live at Camp Dubois, across from St. Louis, Missouri, as they prepare for their journey.

Writing the Journals

President Jefferson had clear goals for the **expedition** Lewis and Clark were about to begin. He told them that they should keep **journals** about their journey. They should write down what they did and saw each day. They should write about animals and plants they saw, American Indians they met, and the land through which they traveled.

Writing materials

The explorers took special care of their writing materials. They stored their materials in waterproof tin boxes. They only took them out for writing. The explorers carried 30 notebooks to write in. Thirteen notebooks were bound in fine red leather. The rest were bound in cloth, elk skin, and other kinds of materials. Some pads of paper were not bound at all.

Lewis and Clark wrote with **quill** pens and ink. The pens were made from the sharpened quill tips of turkey or goose feathers. They used powdered ink, mixing the powder with water.

Lewis and Clark always carried their writing materials with them.

"Having on this day at 4 p.m. completed every arrangement necessary for our departure, we dismissed the barge and crew with orders to return…to St. Louis…confided…likewise our dispatches to the government, letters to our private friends, and a number of articles to the President of the United States."

—*Meriwether Lewis, Wednesday, April 7, 1805*

Journal writing

No one is sure how often Lewis and Clark wrote in the journals. Some people who study history think that Lewis or Clark wrote almost every day. They probably wrote at the end of the day. After making camp, they took a notebook from its waterproof tin box. Someone made ink by mixing ink powder with water in a small container. With a knife, they sharpened the quill of a feather. Then they sat down and wrote.

Five other people in the Corps of Discovery also kept journals. But Lewis and Clark had the most interesting journals.

Know It!

It was easier to travel on rivers than on land. On the Missouri River, the explorers planned to cover between 14 and 20 miles (23 and 32 kilometers) a day.

Pictures and maps

Lewis and Clark also drew pictures and made maps. Lewis knew the most about plants and animals, so he drew the pictures (see pages 32–33). Clark was very good at making maps. He made maps of the Missouri, Columbia, and other rivers in the West. The explorers knew how to tell where they were by the positions of the sun and stars. Then Clark could make maps of their travels.

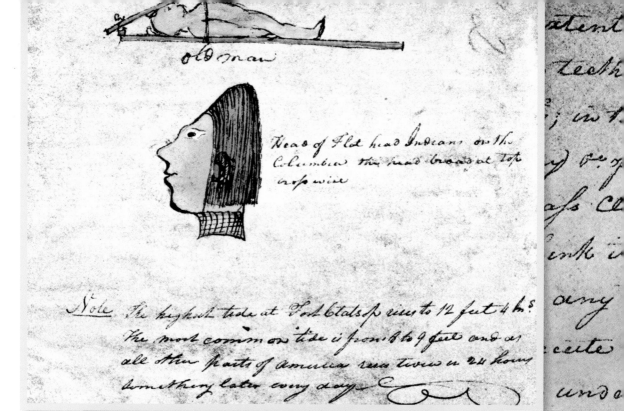

Lewis and Clark encountered many American Indians, including those who used head-flattening devices. Many groups of American Indians practiced head flattening, which did not hurt their heads.

Lewis and Clark wrote about American Indians (see pages 28–31). They told about the different **tribes** in the West and how they lived. They drew pictures of bows and arrows, hatchets, and other things used by the American Indians.

The Journey

The **expedition** set out from near St. Louis on May 14, 1804. The members of the Corps of Discovery traveled in the **keelboat** and two smaller boats called **pirogues**. A pirogue is long and narrow like a canoe. They traveled up the Missouri River.

The Dakotas

By the end of August, the expedition reached the areas that are today North and South Dakota. (For all the parts of the journey, see the map on page 24.) By late October, the explorers found villages of the Hidatsa and Mandan **tribes**.

The Corps needed someone who spoke the language of the Shoshones and other tribes farther west.

The expedition camped for the winter near a Mandan village in North Dakota.

May 14, 1804
The Corps of Discovery leaves the St. Louis area.

late August 1804
The expedition reaches and explores modern-day North and South Dakota.

So they hired French-Canadian fur trapper Toussaint Charbonneau (see the box) and his wife, Sacagawea (see page 29), who was Shoshone, to act as **interpreters**.

In late December, the explorers finished building a camp called Fort Mandan, in present-day North Dakota. It would be their home for the winter of 1804–1805.

"A french man by Name Chabonah [Charbonneau]… visit us, he wished to hire & informed us his 2 Squars [squaws] were Snake [Shoshone] Indians…. [We] engau [engaged] him to go on with us and take one of his wives to interpet the Snake language."

—*William Clark,*
November 4, 1804

Toussaint Charbonneau (1767–about 1843)

Toussaint Charbonneau (pictured above with a red sash around his waste) left Canada to become a fur trader on the Missouri River. He lived with the Hidatsa and Mandan Indians. He had two Shoshone wives. One wife was Sacagawea. Lewis and Clark hired Charbonneau to be an interpreter. Charbonneau knew that Sacagawea could be a great help in talking with the Shoshones near the Rocky Mountains. He made sure she came along.

winter 1804–1805
The expedition sets up a winter camp, called Fort Mandan, in modern-day North Dakota.

Summer travels

By April members of the Corps of Discovery began to head west. On June 13, 1805, the Corps reached the Great Falls of the Missouri River, a series of enormous waterfalls in present-day Montana. By late July, the explorers reached the Three Forks of the Missouri River.

In mid-August, traveling on the Missouri River, the explorers reached the Continental Divide. This is a north–south section of the Rocky Mountains full of dangerous peaks. They managed to pass through it thanks to the Lemhi Pass, a span of land that bridged the gap between the dangerous peaks.

Lewis and Clark had made the important discovery that there was no "northwest passage" to the Pacific. No rivers would allow ships to sail from the East to the West Coast.

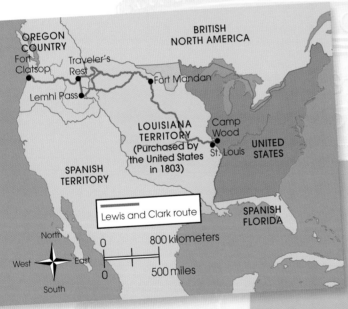

The Lewis and Clark expedition traveled more than 8,000 miles (12,800 kilometers) along rivers and over the Rocky Mountains, traveling to the Pacific Ocean and then back to St. Louis, Missouri.

June 13, 1805
The Corps of Discovery reaches the Great Falls of the Missouri River.

late July 1805
The explorers reach the Three Forks of the Missouri River.

mid-August 1805
The explorers reach the Continental Divide.

Crossing the Bitterroot Mountains was difficult.

Crossing the Bitterroot Mountains

Snow was falling. But the explorers still had to cross a part of the Rocky Mountains called the Bitterroot Mountains. The group almost starved in the mountains. Just in time, they reached the other side. The Nez Perce Indians sold them food.

Reaching the Pacific Ocean

In October the explorers found rivers that flow into the Columbia River. The Columbia River flows to the Pacific Ocean. The explorers built **dugout canoes** and set out.

Lewis and Clark reached the Pacific Ocean on different days in November 1805. They both walked there. The explorers set up winter camp farther inland. They named it Fort Clatsop, after a friendly Indian tribe.

September 1805
The explorers cross the Bitterroot Mountains.

October 1805
The explorers discover rivers that flow into the Columbia River.

November 1805
Lewis and Clark reach the Pacific Ocean. They set up Fort Clatsop.

This statue of Lewis and Clark, called "The Captain's Return" was dedicated on September 23, 2006—the 200th anniversary of their return.

Heading home

The explorers began their journey back home to St. Louis in March 1806. For the journey back home, Lewis and Clark learned some shortcuts from the American Indians. The expedition split into two groups at Traveler's Rest, a spot they set up in present-day Montana (see the map on page 24).

Clark took one group to explore the Yellowstone River. Lewis took the other group on a shortcut to the Missouri River. The two groups met on the Missouri River. They all headed for St. Louis. On the way, they left Charbonneau and Sacagawea at their home with the Mandan Indians.

York

York was the expedition's only African American. York was a **slave** who belonged to Clark. York had some freedoms on the journey. He carried a gun, and he voted on where to spend winters.

March 1806
The Corps of Discovery begins the journey back to St. Louis.

Welcomed as heroes

The explorers were greeted as heroes when they reached St. Louis in September 1806. Many people thought that Lewis and Clark had died in the wilderness, but President Jefferson did not. Lewis took the **journals** to Washington, D.C. He gave them to President Jefferson.

Settlers head west

Many **pioneers** followed the route of Lewis and Clark. People from the East began settling the West. They traveled by boat on the Missouri River. They traveled by wagon over what was known as the Oregon Trail. Thanks to this expedition, the United States would eventually claim the Oregon **Territory** in the Pacific Northwest (see the box).

Know It!

The Oregon Territory became the states of Idaho, Oregon, and Washington. Parts of Montana and Wyoming were also once part of the Oregon Territory.

This illustration shows pioneers in covered wagons on the Oregon Trail, passing through Wyoming along the Sweetwater River.

September 1806
The explorers are welcomed in St. Louis.

27

Writing About American Indians

Over the course of their **expedition**, Lewis, Clark, and the other members of the Corps of Discovery learned about far more than routes and rivers.

President Jefferson had told Lewis and Clark to learn about American Indians they met. Jefferson wanted U.S. fur traders to go farther west. He told Lewis and Clark to promise the American Indians guns and other goods if they welcomed the traders.

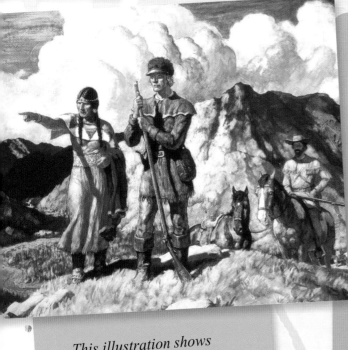

This illustration shows Sacagawea guiding Lewis and Clark.

"The Indian woman [Sacagawea] recognized the point of a high plain to our right which she informed us was not very distant from the summer retreat of her nation on a river beyond the mountains which runs to the west.... She assures us that we shall either find her people [the Shoshone] on this river or on the river immediately west."

—*Meriwether Lewis,*
Thursday, August 8, 1805

Meeting the Indians

During their expedition, Lewis and Clark met about 50 **tribes** of American Indians. The explorers explained that the United States now owned the land, and that Jefferson was their "Great Father."

One of the most helpful American Indians they met was Sacagawea (see the box). She helped the explorers trade for horses. On the journey, she also helped them find plants that they could eat. Sometimes she helped them find their way.

Sacagawea was honored on this U.S. postage stamp in 1994.

Sacagawea (1788–1812)

Sacagawea was the daughter of a Shoshone chief. Hidatsa warriors captured her and took her from her home in the Rockies. They sold her to the Mandans, who sold her to her husband, Toussaint Charbonneau (see page 23). Sacagawea was still a teenager when she set off with the explorers. She took her newborn son along.

Friendly and hostile meetings

Most of the American Indians that the explorers met where friendly. But some meetings were tense. A band of Teton Sioux that the explorers encountered in September 1804 wanted one of the boats. A chief stepped in and avoided a fight.

The helpful Shoshones sold the explorers horses for crossing mountains. The Clatsop Indians in Oregon helped the expedition survive the winter of 1805–1806. The Nez Perce, who lived west of the Rockies, also helped the explorers. The Nez Perce let the explorers stay with them until the snow in the Bitterroot Mountains had melted (see page 25).

This illustration shows Lewis meeting the Shoshones.

The Nez Perce also showed the explorers how to make a **dugout canoe** from a tree trunk. They set a fire in the center of the log. Then they scraped away the charcoal and ashes. They did this over and over until they had a hollowed out log that served as a canoe.

"Children I take you all by the hand as the children of your Great father the President of the U. States of America who is the great chief of all the white people.… Children Your Great father…has derected me to inform his red children to be at peace with each other, and the white people who may come into your country"

—*undated speech by Clark*

Writing About Nature

Some of the most interesting writings in the **journals** of Lewis and Clark were about nature. The explorers wrote about 178 plants and 122 animals that scientists had not known about before.

Know It!

The plant **specimens** that Lewis and Clark collected are **primary sources.** Researchers can see the plants at the Academy of Natural Sciences in Philadelphia.

"In the evening we saw a Brown or Grisley beare on a sand beech, I went out with one man Geo Drewyer & Killed the bear, which was verry large and a turrible looking animal, which we found verry hard to kill we Shot ten Balls into him before we killed him."

—*William Clark,*
Sunday, May 5, 1805

Small and large animals

One of the animals they found was the prairie dog. These small rodents make a sound like a barking dog. Prairie dogs dig burrows underground. Hundreds of prairie dogs live in one underground "town." Other animals frightened the explorers. Grizzly bears looking for food attacked members of the **expedition**.

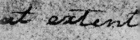

The size and strength of grizzly bears amazed the explorers.

Whenever they could, Lewis and Clark saved the skin or skeleton of an animal to bring back to President Jefferson. These real-life examples are called specimens.

Describing plants

Lewis described trees, grasses, and flowers that he saw. He carefully wrote down every detail about a plant, such as the Pacific yew. He told where the plant grew. The explorers also collected plant specimens.

Weather in the West

Lewis and Clark were the first people to make a scientific study of the weather in the West. They used Fahrenheit thermometers to measure the temperature of the air. They wrote down the temperature at sunrise and at 4:00 p.m. They recorded temperatures every day from September 19, 1804, to September 6, 1805. That day, they broke their last thermometer. It broke while they were climbing the Bitterroot Mountains in deep snow.

Lewis and Clark also noted in their journals whether the day was sunny or stormy. They wrote which direction the wind was blowing. They recorded how much rain or snow fell.

Charting rivers

Lewis and Clark made maps of the rivers. They found **tributaries**, which are streams that feed into a larger river. They found out how far each river or stream went.

Know It!

During their journey, the explorers had to cross the dangerous mountains of the Continental Divide (see page 24). Rivers on the west side of the Continental Divide flow to the West. On the east side of the Continental Divide, rivers flow to the East.

They were especially interested in the Missouri River, since it was the main route to the West. The explorers measured how deep the Missouri River was at different places. They also measured how fast the **current** flowed. They had thought that the Columbia and other rivers on the west side of the Rockies were small streams. They were surprised to discover that they were in fact big rivers.

A journal page shows a drawing of a Coho salmon from a western river.

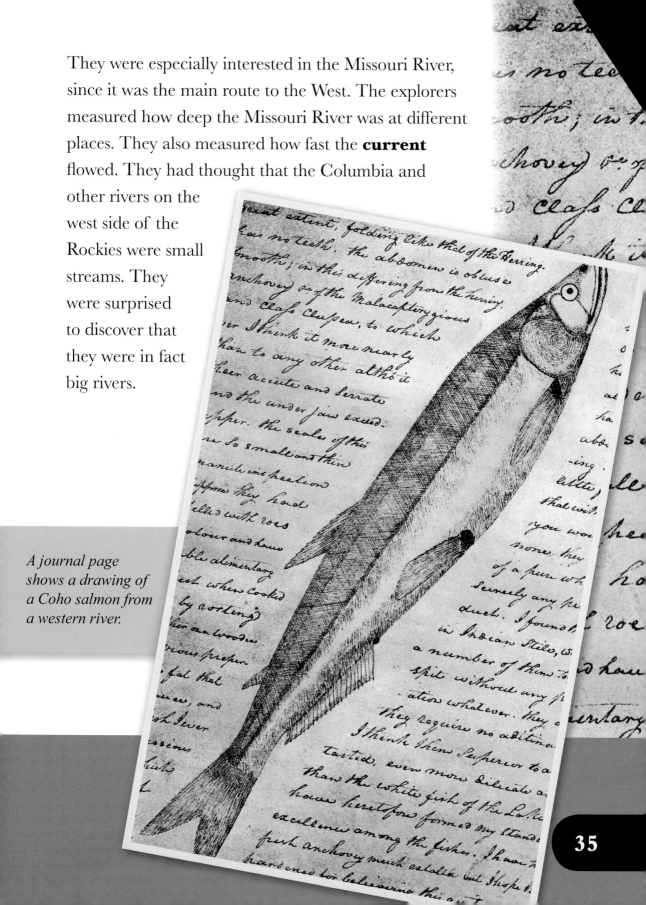

Journey of the Journals

After Lewis and Clark returned from their exhibition, President Jefferson requested the original copies of their **journals** be kept at the American Philosophical Society (APS) in Philadelphia, Pennsylvania.

Publishing the journals

Lewis and Clark wanted their journals to be published as a book. But some of the **entries** were hard to understand. They needed to be **edited**.

Lewis had the best writing skills so he was a good choice to get the journals ready to be published. But Lewis had little time. In 1807 President Jefferson made Lewis governor of the Louisiana **Territory**. Lewis died in 1809 before getting to do any work on the journals.

The American Philosophical Society building houses the journals of Lewis and Clark.

Clark did not work on the journals, either. He did not have good writing skills. There are many misspelled words in his journal entries. He had others do the editing. These editors corrected words misspelled by Clark. They also checked dates of journal entries and other facts in the journals. Some editors inserted footnotes to explain anything that might look like an error.

Early editions

Various editors produced many **editions** of the journals during the 1800s and the 1900s. The first book about the journals came out in 1814. It was the only one for 80 years.

In the 1890s, a doctor and bird expert named Elliott Coues borrowed the journals from the APS. He took the actual journals out of their **archive** in Philadelphia. He brought them to Washington, D.C. Coues used the journals to write the second book about the **expedition**.

1809
Lewis dies. Clark is left to handle publishing the journals.

1814
The first book of the journals is published.

A valuable copy

Coues made a book that contained a lot of valuable information about the expedition and its findings. For example, he made a list of all the topics covered in the journals.

Coues also damaged the journals. He cut some pages up. He put some pages in a different order. Fortunately, he had an exact copy made of the journals before he began his work. The copy was stored in boxes at a publishing company and almost forgotten. It was found about 70 years later. This valuable copy showing how the original journals looked is now kept at Lewis & Clark University in Portland, Oregon.

Elliot Coues made lots of changes to the original Lewis and Clark journals.

1890s
Elliott Coues uses the original journals to write a book about the expedition.

The Nebraska edition

Most scholars think that the best edition of the journals today is called the Nebraska edition. It was made by a team of editors and computer programmers at the University of Nebraska in Lincoln.

The Nebraska team began working on the Lewis and Clark journals in 1979. They did not finish until 1999, 20 years after they started. The team had many problems to solve. One big problem was all the oddly spelled words.

The Nebraska edition contains about 5,000 pages. Some of these pages explain entries in the journal. It also contains journals kept by other members of the Corps of Discovery.

Computer programmers put the Nebraska edition online. They scanned the actual pages written by Lewis and Clark. You can go to the website (see page 47) and read the exact words of Lewis and Clark. You can see their maps and drawings.

Know It!

An exact copy of the Lewis and Clark journals is about a million words long.

1999
The Nebraska Edition of the journals is published.

The Journals of Lewis and Clark Today

The original **journals** are still kept in a **vault** at the American Philosophical Society in Philadelphia, safe from fire and moisture. The pages are stored in special acid-free boxes. Paper and cardboard containing acid can ruin documents such as the journals.

Keeping the journals safe

Archivists, people who look after valuable historical documents, take care of the journals. Archivists sometimes wear gloves when they handle valuable **primary source** documents. However, archivists do not wear gloves when handling the Lewis and Clark journals, because the gloves might harm the material that the explorers wrote on.

Some of the Lewis and Clark journals are on display in a glass case at the American Philosophical Society. In addition, the APS sells facsimiles of three volumes of the journals. A facsimile is an exact copy of a document showing how the original looked.

Seeing the journals online

In the past, a researcher who wanted to study the journals had to go to Philadelphia and ask permission from the APS archivists. When researchers want to study the journals now, however, they can see online images of pages made by the APS or University of Nebraska scholars and computer programmers.

Celebrating Lewis and Clark

The years 2003 to 2006 marked the bicentennial (200th anniversary) of the Lewis and Clark **expedition**. The expedition and the journals that the explorers kept inspired many celebrations and monuments.

The Lewis and Clark Trail

The U.S. government established the Lewis and Clark National Historic Trail. Special markers identify sites along the route that Lewis and Clark traveled.

Replicas and reenactments

A replica of Fort Mandan, where the expedition spent the winter of 1804-05, was built along the Missouri River in North Dakota. Visitor's centers at other places along the route tell about Lewis and Clark's meetings with different **tribes** of American Indians.

The 200th anniversary of Lewis and Clark's journey inspired many students to learn about this time in American history. The lesson plans, historic places along the route, replicas, and reenactments continue today. And these journals continue to be a valuable primary source that tells about the time in America's history when the young nation grew rapidly into the Wild West.

The city of St. Louis celebrated the bicentennial of the return of Lewis and Clark from their journey with fireworks.

2003-2006
Bicentennial celebrations
honor the expedition.

Timeline

1800
Spain promises the Louisiana Territory to France in a secret treaty.

1801
Thomas Jefferson becomes the third president of the United States.

April 30, 1803
France sells the Louisiana Territory to the United States for $15 million.

May 14, 1804
The Corps of Discovery leaves the St. Louis area.

winter 1803–04
Lewis, Clark, and their crew live at Camp DuBois, across from St. Louis, Missouri, as they prepare for their journey.

late August 1804
The expedition reaches and explores modern-day North and South Dakota.

winter 1804–05
The expedition sets up a winter camp, called Fort Mandan, in modern-day North Dakota.

June 13, 1805
The Corps of Discovery reaches the Great Falls of the Missouri River.

September 1806
The explorers are welcomed in St. Louis.

March 1806
The Corps of Discovery begins the journey back to St. Louis.

1809
Lewis dies. Clark is left to handle publishing the journals.

1814
The first book of the journals is published.

1890s
Elliott Coues uses the original journals to write a book about the expedition.

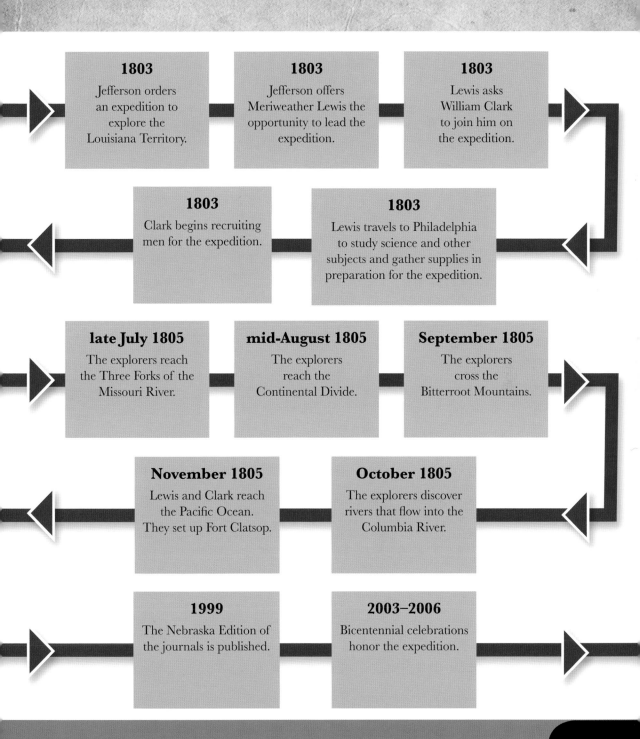

1803
Jefferson orders an expedition to explore the Louisiana Territory.

1803
Jefferson offers Meriweather Lewis the opportunity to lead the expedition.

1803
Lewis asks William Clark to join him on the expedition.

1803
Clark begins recruiting men for the expedition.

1803
Lewis travels to Philadelphia to study science and other subjects and gather supplies in preparation for the expedition.

late July 1805
The explorers reach the Three Forks of the Missouri River.

mid-August 1805
The explorers reach the Continental Divide.

September 1805
The explorers cross the Bitterroot Mountains.

November 1805
Lewis and Clark reach the Pacific Ocean. They set up Fort Clatsop.

October 1805
The explorers discover rivers that flow into the Columbia River.

1999
The Nebraska Edition of the journals is published.

2003–2006
Bicentennial celebrations honor the expedition.

Glossary

archive place that holds a collection of historical documents and other primary sources

archivist person in charge of historical documents

colony area controlled by another country

current water moving in a direction

dugout canoe canoe made from a hollowed out log

edit prepare the final content of a book or article

edition version of a published book or other work

entry item written in a diary or journal

expedition journey by a group of people for a specific purpose

interpreter person who can translate from one spoken language into another

journal daily record of events

keelboat large, flat-bottomed boat for carrying freight on rivers

pioneer one of the first people to settle an area

pirogue long, narrow, lightweight boat or canoe

plantation large farm where crops are grown to be sold

primary source document or object made in the past that provides information about a certain time

produce fruits, vegetables, and other items grown on farms

quill hollow shaft of a feather used for writing with ink

secondary source account written by someone who studied primary sources

slave person who is forced to work for someone against his or her will

specimen individual example of a species or mineral

territory geographic area belonging to or under control of a government

treaty legal agreement between nations

tribe social group that shares the same language, customs, and beliefs

tributary river or stream that flows into a larger river

vault room used for safely storing items

Find Out More

Books

Berne, Emma Carlson. *Sacagawea: Crossing the Continent with Lewis & Clark.* New York: Sterling, 2010.

Eubank, Patricia Reeder. *Seaman's Journal: On the Trail with Lewis and Clark.* Nashville, Tenn.: Ideals, 2002.

Meloche, Renee. *Meriwether Lewis: Journey Across America.* Austin, Tex.: Emerald Books, 2006.

Perritano, John. *The Lewis and Clark Expedition.* New York: Children's Press, 2010.

Websites

http://lewisandclarkjournals.unl.edu/
Lewis & Clark Journals Online: Nebraska Edition
Read the journals on the University of Nebraska Lincoln's website.

www.nationalgeographic.com/lewisandclark/index.html
National Geographic Interactive Feature
Experience some of the journey at this website.

www.nationalgeographic.com/west/index.html
National Geographic Kids Game: Go West Across America with Lewis and Clark
Choose your own westward adventure at this website!

www.pbs.org/lewisandclark/
PBS: Lewis and Clark
This site is a companion to the Ken Burns film about the Lewis and Clark expedition.

Index